GREENLAND   ARCTIC OCEAN

NORTH AMERICA

UNITED STATES

San Francisco

Independence

Boston
New York

New Orleans

San Blas

Acapulco

ATLANTIC OCEAN

EUROPE

AFRICA

SOUTH AMERICA

Callao

Rio de Janeiro

Valparaiso

Cape Horn

N
W   E
S

To Barbara—
and with thanks to all of
the helpful people I met while traveling
through the goldfields
of California.

Copyright © 1999 Rosalyn Schanzer

LIBRARY OF CONGRESS CATALOGING-IN-PUBLICATION DATA
Gold Fever! Tales from the California Gold Rush/ [compiled] by Rosalyn Schanzer.
  p.   cm.
Summary: Uses lighthearted illustrations and excerpts from letters, journals,
  and newspaper articles to relate the story of the California Gold Rush of 1848.
  ISBN 0-7922-7303-6
1. California—Gold discoveries—Sources—Juvenile literature. 2. California—
History—1846–1850—Sources—Juvenile literature. [1. California—Gold discoveries.
2. California—History—1846–1850.]   I. Schanzer, Rosalyn.
F865.G64   1999
979.4'04—dc21   98–20790

Printed in U.S.A.

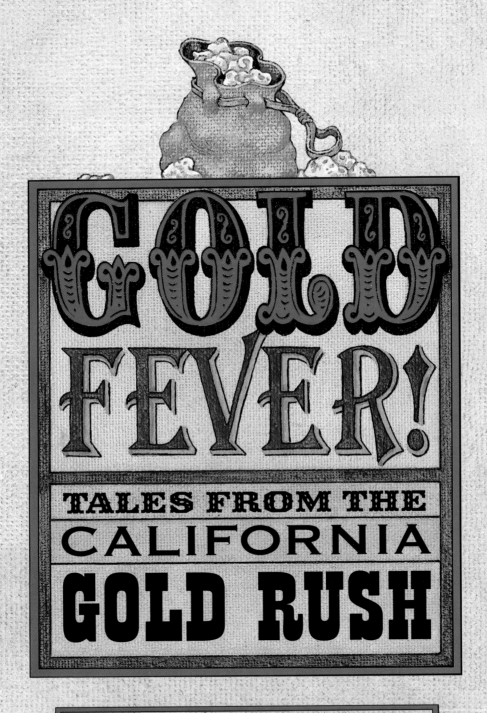

GOLD FEVER!

TALES FROM THE
CALIFORNIA
GOLD RUSH

ROSALYN SCHANZER

NATIONAL GEOGRAPHIC SOCIETY

Washington, D.C.

AN ASTOUNDING DISCOVERY

MARSHALL'S
~ OWN ~
ACCOUNT

JOHN SUTTER
*A wealthy landowner
near Coloma, California*

JAMES MARSHALL
*A carpenter
hired by Sutter*

MARCH 1847
Mr. Sutter wanted to find a good site for a sawmill. I traveled along the river the whole way until I reached the exact spot we were hunting.

AUGUST 1847
Digging the foundation of the mill we cut some distance into soft granite, and a ditch was cut in the rear of the mill.

JANUARY 24, 1848
It was a clear cold morning I shall never forget—my eye was caught with the glimpse of something shining in the bottom of the ditch. I reached my hand down and picked it up; it made my heart thump, for I was certain it was gold. Then I saw another piece. Putting one of the pieces on a hard river stone, I took another and commenced hammering. It was soft and didn't break; it therefore must be **GOLD**!!!

In three or four days we had picked up about three ounces. In about a week's time I took all that we had collected to Mr. Sutter, who at once declared it was gold.

We soon ciphered that there was no silver or copper in the gold, but that it was entirely pure. In a very short time we discovered that the whole country was but one bed of gold— a discovery that hasn't been of much benefit to me.

CALIFORNIAN
March 15, 1848
(from back page of the newspaper)

GOLD MINE FOUND—
In the newly made raceway of the sawmill recently erected by Captain Sutter on the American Fork, gold has been found in considerable quantities.

OREGON SPECTATOR
End of 1848

Almost the entire male population has gone gold digging in California.

NEW YORK HERALD
January 1849

The great discovery of gold has thrown the American people in a state of the wildest excitement. Gold can be scooped up in pans at the rate of a pound of pure dust a scoop. 'Ho! For California' is the cry everywhere.

HO! FOR CALIFORNIA

The blacksmith dropped his hammer, the carpenter his plane, the mason his trowel, the farmer his sickle, the baker his loaf, and the tapster his bottle. All were off for the mines, some on horses, some on carts, and some on crutches, and one went in a litter. REVEREND WALTER COLTON

The big excitement swept all Tennessee like a fire in prairie grass. Every loose-footed man wanted to go. Some men that was tied with families actually set down and cried 'cause they couldn't go. J. H. BEADLE

Passed through large schools of flying fish. One paid us a visit.
The ocean being so smooth, many of us plunged overboard for a swim.

RICHARD LUNT HALE

I am all out of patience and was never so heartily sick of cards in my life, for
it is nothing else from morning til night. JOHN J. CRAVEN

At six p.m. made the island of Santa Catherina. The natives in their
little boats thronged the sides of the brig with all kinds of fruit for sale.
But the cry of 'Gold!' 'Gold!' is on the air, and every delay, no matter
how pleasant, makes us impatient. RICHARD LUNT HALE

WE ROUND CAPE HORN

Cape Horn must be weathered! It makes me shiver. Sudden squalls, gales, hail, sleet, rain coming without warning and disappearing in the same mysterious way. We have passed several vessels, all heading for the goldfields. RICHARD LUNT HALE

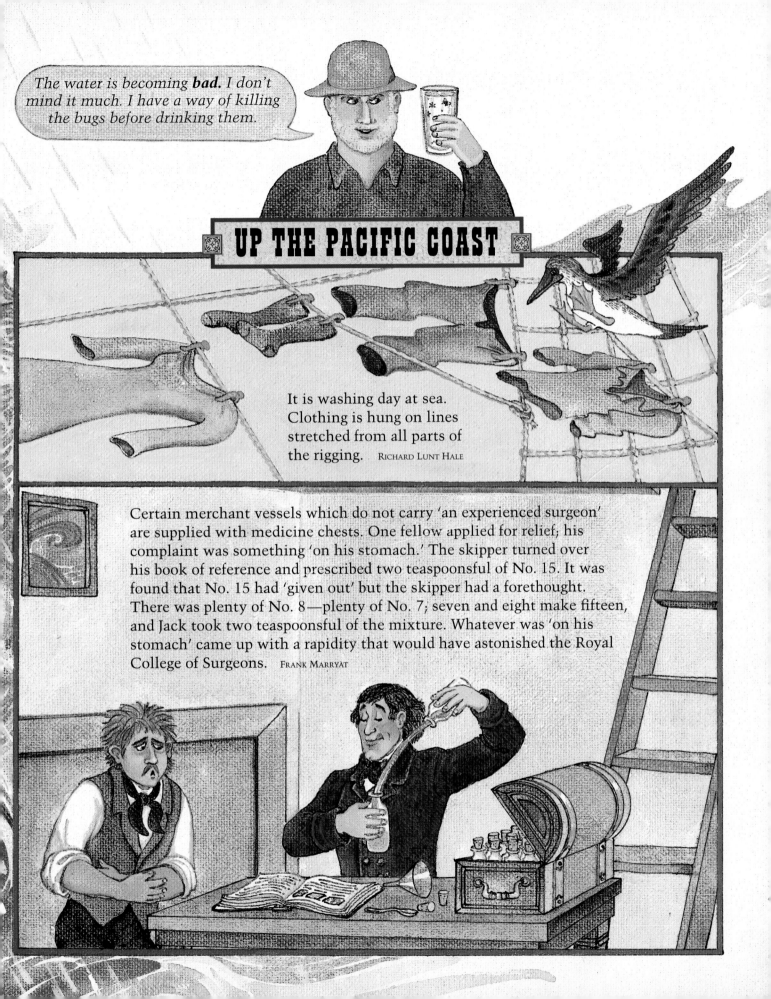

The water is becoming **bad.** I don't mind it much. I have a way of killing the bugs before drinking them.

UP THE PACIFIC COAST

It is washing day at sea. Clothing is hung on lines stretched from all parts of the rigging. RICHARD LUNT HALE

Certain merchant vessels which do not carry 'an experienced surgeon' are supplied with medicine chests. One fellow applied for relief; his complaint was something 'on his stomach.' The skipper turned over his book of reference and prescribed two teaspoonsful of No. 15. It was found that No. 15 had 'given out' but the skipper had a forethought. There was plenty of No. 8—plenty of No. 7; seven and eight make fifteen, and Jack took two teaspoonsful of the mixture. Whatever was 'on his stomach' came up with a rapidity that would have astonished the Royal College of Surgeons. FRANK MARRYAT

VIA THE PANAMA SHORTCUT

We shall go up the Chagres River for about 75 miles, then take mules for 24 miles, then a large steamer for San Francisco which will take about 30 days if we have good luck. JENNIE MEGQUIER

The air was filled with the music of birds, the chattering of monkeys, parrots in any quantity, alligators lying on the banks too lazy to move. JENNIE MEGQUIER

We entered this noble bay
with a cracking breeze among
a forest of shipping. FRANKLIN A. BUCK

THE JOURNEY OVERLAND

A company of forty of us started at Independence, Missouri. The whole country was under water. The mud was thicker and stickier every day; but the men kept a-hoopin' and swearin' and I never seed men so crazy to git on. J. H. BEADLE

OVERLAND ROUTES

NORTH AMERICA

SAN FRANCISCO   INDEPENDENCE

Pacific Ocean   Atlantic Ocean

Gulf of Mexico

Our route today has been over rough prairie with little gullies ten or twelve feet deep through which our wagon had to plunge. ELISHA DOUGLASS PERKINS

For six hours traveled over the most perfectly flat country ever conceived of. Nothing was in sight but the green of the prairie and the blue of the sky. ELISHA DOUGLASS PERKINS

This morning antelope are running round us in all directions and such running! They glide at a bird's pace. ELISHA DOUGLASS PERKINS

Hail exceeded anything I ever saw, being as large as pigeon eggs. Found our cookstove full of water. There may be fun in camping, but we haven't discovered any. ELISHA DOUGLASS PERKINS

The oldest of the men who had joined the company complained of intense pain and sickness, and was soon obliged to lie down in the wagon. In two or three hours the poor old man expired. The wind moaned and rain fell. I could not sleep. Indians built a fire, chanting hour after hour. I knew it was a death dirge.

SARAH ROYCE

We made our way to the very edge of the cliff and looked down. We were gone so long that the train was stopped and men sent out in search of us.   SALLIE HESTER, AGE 14

Roads are rocky and the dust is horrible. The men wear veils tied over their hats as a protection. When we reach camp at night, they are covered with dust from head to heels.   SALLIE HESTER

Grasshoppers et our team of mules and then pitched horseshoes for the wagon.

When men are tired and dirty they'll quarrel about anything.   J. H. BEADLE

For the first time in my life I saw a mirage; it was a small lake seen through openings in a row of trees. But as day dawned, these beautiful sights disappeared. We were now miles out on the desert without a mouthful of food for the cattle and only two or three quarts of water in a little cask. The old man who had been traveling with us had a small straw mattress. A small portion of it was dealt out to the cattle to keep the poor things from starving.   SARAH ROYCE

Any man who makes a trip by land deserves to find a fortune.
ALONZO DELANO

When we got to the Carson River there was sweet clean water
and grass and trees. Our men ran right into the water and
swallowed and swallowed til they staggered like drunk men.
We was into Californy at last, and it looked like heaven.   J. H. BEADLE

OFF TO THE DIGGINGS

Armed with a pickax, shovel, hoe, and rifle, I found myself wending my way to the golden hills.   E. G. BUFFRAM

Below us the swift river glided. On the banks was a village of canvas bleached to perfection and miners waist-deep in the water, entrenched in holes like gravediggers, on the brink of the stream washing out 'prospects' from tin pans, or coyoteing in holes from which their heads popped out like squirrels. All was merriment, vigor, and determination.

FRANK MARRYAT

What a lovely sight greeted our eyes. It was worth the whole wearisome journey, danger from Indians, grizzly bears, sleeping under the stars and all to behold this beautiful vision.

DAME SHIRLEY
(LOUISE AMELIA KNAPP SMITH CLAPP)

When I first saw men carrying heavy stones in the sun, standing nearly waist-deep in water, and grubbing with their hands in the gravel and clay, there seemed little temptation to gold digging; but when the shining particles were poured out lavishly from a tin basin, I confess there was a sudden itching in my fingers. BAYARD TAYLOR

I trudged merrily away to a ravine, and there at the bottom, strewn against the whole length of the rock was bright yellow gold, in little pieces about the size and shape of a grain of barley. EUREKA! Oh how my heart beat! E. G. BUFFRAM

Here was the gold. All you had to do was get it out!
FRANK MARRYAT

We found the gold on the Yuba exceedingly fine. We inquired to the washers of their success. Seeing that we were 'green horns,' they told us direct lies. E. G. Buffram

Mother wants to know who does our washing. We wash our own clothes and our own faces and when we don't choose to, we go with dirty clothes and dirty faces too. Last winter we got a woman to wash our clothes but now there is not a woman within nineteen miles of us. Charles Bush

Notice was given that 'on Sunday the famous grizzly bear "America" would fight a wild bull. Admission, $5.'

FRANK MARRYAT

Miners' entire subsistence upon salt meat without vegetable matter produced land scurvy. Many died. I noticed its first attack upon myself by swelling and bleeding of gums, followed by swellings of both legs, which rendered me unable to walk. Growing daily weaker, I was almost in despair. My limbs were turning completely black.

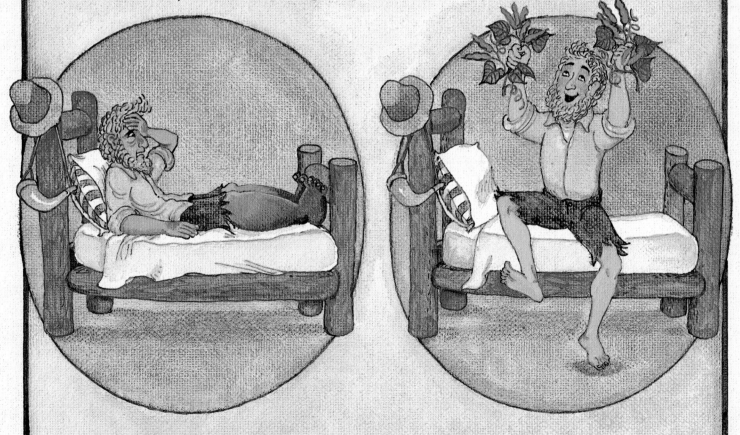

I believe I should have died had not one of our party out deer-hunting found a quantity of beans which sprouted from the ground. These seemed to operate magically, and in a week, I found myself able to walk. E. G. BUFFRAM

GOOD NEWS

One character known as 'Buckshot' lived alone in a small tent.
His tastes were luxurious; the finest hams, preserved oysters, corn and
peas, Chinese sweetmeats and dried fruits were all at his table, and dinner
was moistened by champagne. He was reported to have dug between
thirty and forty thousand dollars. BAYARD TAYLOR

Last week a German boy named Fritz and
a colored man named Duff found a block
of gold-bearing quartz weighing 193 pounds.
Value from $5,000 to $10,000.

NEWSPAPER IN MARIPOSA

I met a man today in patched buckskins
rough as a badger from his hole, who
had $15,000 in yellow dust swung at his
back. REVEREND WALTER COLTON

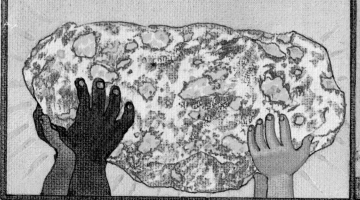

CALIFORNIA PLEASURES

SAN FRANCISCO

On every side stood buildings covered with signs in all languages. Great quantities of goods piled up in the open air, and streets were full of Yankees, Californians in serapes and sombreros, Chileans, Sonorans, Kanakas from Hawaii, Chinese, and others impossible to recognize. BAYARD TAYLOR

CARPENTER SHOP

JOSEPH'S

EMPORIUM

CANDLE & SOAP WORKS

BARBER SHOP

FANCY GOODS

FINE HATS

DRUG STORE

CULINARY SUPPLY

MINING IMPLEMENTS

RICE

合華

歡迎參觀

The banks are very crowded, and full of tobacco smoke. Instead of the chinking of money, you hear thumps on the counter, as large leathern bags of gold dust come down on it. FRANK MARRYAT

San Francisco was peopled by men alone! He who cannot make a bed, cook a beefsteak, or sew up his own rips and rents is unfit to be a citizen of California. BAYARD TAYLOR

You may get an excellent beefsteak and a cup of good coffee or chocolate, but milk, fruit and vegetables are luxuries, and fresh butter is rarely heard of. BAYARD TAYLOR

NIGHT LIFE

Commercial Street, which is composed entirely of saloons, is a blaze of light, and resounds with music from one end to the other. FRANK MARRYAT

A female violinist tasks her talent. A musician has a set of Pandean pipes fastened at his chin, a drum on his back, and cymbals in his hands. There is a full band of Ethiopian serenaders. BAYARD TAYLOR

They are playing monte, the favorite game in California. The dealer throws out his cards with a cool, nonchalant air. BAYARD TAYLOR

Amidst all the turmoil and noisy music, two or three reports of a pistol startle the stranger and crack the mirror on the other side of him.

FRANK MARRYAT

MAKING MONEY

Everyone must do something; it matters but very little what it is; if they stick to it, they are bound to make money. JENNIE MEGQUIER

I was satisfied that I could make paper and pencil much more profitable tools to work with than a pick and shovel.

J. D. BORTHWICK, ARTIST, WRITER, AND FAILED MINER

We had on deck 4 houses. They cost $147 apiece and we have sold them for $4,000 and got the dust. I have no desire to go to the diggings. As long as the gold mines last, business will be good. FRANKLIN A. BUCK

We fitted up our store, carpeted it with Chinese mats, furnished it with chairs and tables, and live in luxury. We sold $1,500 worth of goods in one day. The first dust I received, $2,800, made my eyes sparkle as I spooned it into a pail. But now, I weigh it out with as little feeling as I would so much sand. FRANKLIN A. BUCK

$100
Mayfield .42 caliber whiskey

~PAPER~
$1.50°° PER SHEET

1 TACK $.10°°

CHINESE LAUNDRY
~12 SHIRTS~
washed and ironed for
$3.°°

When gold was first discovered, Indians would exchange handfuls of it for any food they desired or for any garment gaudy enough to tickle their fancy. Latterly, they have become more careful, placing on the palm of the hand perhaps a teaspoonful of gold dust.

E. G. BUFFRAM

We purchased 200 pounds of flour for $300, 100 pounds of pork for $200, and sugar and coffee at $1 a pound. At these prices, the trader realized a greater profit from the miner's labor than the miner did. E. G. BUFFRAM

The Chinese are the greatest traders in the world. They can calculate how much a bill of goods comes to in their heads, and they are first-rate cooks. FRANKLIN A. BUCK

BOOMTOWNS

CHICKEN THIEF FLAT

MAD MULE GULCH

GROUND HOG'S GLORY

SKINFLINT

FLEA TOWN

GOUGE EYE

GRIZZLY FLAT

BOGUS THUNDER

JACKASS GULCH

POVERTY HILL

GIT-UP-AND-GIT

CUT THROAT

RAT TRAP SLIDE

ONE EYE

RATTLESNAKE DIGGINGS

In Stockton we slept on barrel stays with scanty blankets and well filled with athletic and courageous and determined fleas.

HORACE C. SNOW

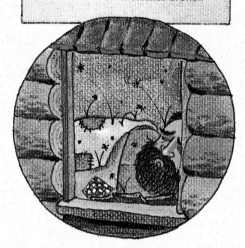

This is a funny-looking town anyway. Nearly everybody is up to their knees in mud and water. Snakes are plenty. They come down the river, crawl under our beds, and everywhere.

SALLIE HESTER IN VERNON, CALIFORNIA

It is a wild and romantic scene. We bake pancakes, fry pork, drink coffee, and sleep on the ground. Wolves stole some meat from a neighbor's tent, taking it from within a foot or two of his head. HIRAM PIERCE

Do you have any food? We will gladly pay!

We met a forlorn group with rags fastened round their blistered feet, trying to force on their skeleton animals. They inquired for bread and meat and seemed anxious to pay. This company had over $100,000 in gold. One had the largest lump that had yet been found; it weighed over 20 pounds. Yet what is gold where there is nothing to eat? REVEREND WALTER COLTON

Chickens were persistent gatherers of small nuggets of gold, and their gizzards were regularly searched by the cooks who prepared them for the oven. At Diamond Springs one was killed for a Sunday dinner whose gizzard panned out at $12.80.

CHARLES PETERS

Funds beautifully reduced. We resolved—out of respect for the pocket—to commence the art of living without eating. HORACE C. SNOW

THE WHEELS OF CHANGE

Many a time I've seen a man go off with a little money and never be seen alive. It got so that there was men that would cut a throat for ten dollars. Everybody carried the irons with him ready to pop at a minute's notice. If it was known a man was going to leave, it was s'posed he'd made his pile and had it with him. At last I made a little raise and concluded to come home. Me and my partner just laid down our tools one night right where we worked, and when the camp was asleep lit out over the hills 'thout saying a word. Got home round by Panama, and when I figured up, I was just three hundred ahead on the three years trip. Better stayed at home.

J. P. BEADLE

LAND OF ABUNDANCE

This place is getting so civilized that I have nothing to write. A fight is rare; gambling does not attract any attention as people are not so flush with money as they used to be. No scandal or elopements—the doctor says it is distressingly healthy, owing to people drinking less whiskey and keeping better homes. FRANKLIN A. BUCK, JANUARY 22, 1860

Gold is not the only product of California. Her fertile valleys and rich plains are capable of producing untold agricultural wealth. Her lofty pines and spreading oaks afford abundant material. Her thousand streams furnish inexhaustible water power, and her forests, mountains, and lakes abound with game. E. G. BUFFRAM

Let the farmer come,
and from the abundant soil
produce the necessities of life.

————◆————

Let the mechanic and laborer come,
and build up the towns.

————◆————

Let the ladies come,
and with their smiles
bring happiness into
the wilderness.

E. G. Buffram

A NOTE FROM THE AUTHOR

For centuries, Indian children in California had used shimmering yellow rocks as skipping stones in the streams of the Sierra Nevada and had taken little notice of the glittery flecks sparkling from crevices and gullies and river banks. But this remote and sleepy land of Mexicans, Spanish missionaries, and Indians collided head-on with the future on the chilly morning of January 24, 1848, when carpenter James Marshall first spotted a pea-size piece of gold in the American River near a mill he was building. His discovery set off one of the greatest mass migrations in the history of the world.

Gold fever had struck, and it spread like wildfire. Frenzied adventurers from more than 70 nations around the world gleefully stampeded to California to find their fortunes.

◆————◆

What kinds of people were the gold seekers? How did they reach California, and what did they have to say about their great adventure? It seems to me that there is no better way to answer such questions than to let these men and women and children tell their tales in their own words, and they have plenty of tales to tell. Enormous volumes of their lively, informative, and often hilarious letters, journals, and newspaper articles are still available and make the California gold rush and its adventurous participants spring vividly to life.

◆————◆

To write this book, I gleaned many of my favorite anecdotes, making sure to include stories that followed a sequential history of the period. I tried to use exact quotes as much as possible, although some archaic phrases and lengthy passages have been deleted to make reading easier for a young audience. For the same reason, I have omitted ellipses and used some modern spellings and capitalizations. Most of the quotes are attributed to real people; the few unattributed quotes are, to the best of my knowledge, anonymous or represent versions of popular tales from the period.

The pictures for this book were painted on rough canvas with acrylics. Before starting my sketches, I traveled to California and visited every mining site, museum, and mining town that I could find. I took more than 600 photographs of everything from gold nuggets and mining equipment to saloons and scenery so that my pictures could be as accurate as possible. I also discovered a great number of drawings, paintings, photographs, and political cartoons made during the period. These helped me figure out what kinds of clothes the miners wore (lots of red shirts and exotic attire from all over the globe). I could see what the ships looked like and how the covered wagons were furnished.

I learned a lot about the attitudes of participants from their words and from images made during the gold rush era.

———◆———

What ever happened to the players in this tale? Many participants did not fare well. "What a great misfortune was this sudden discovery of gold for me," bemoaned John Sutter, on whose huge estate gold was first discovered. He lost his shirt when all his workers ran off to look for gold, and he had to sell off his property. James Marshall, who first discovered the gold, had no further luck at mining and died a poor blacksmith in 1885. Many other disillusioned fortune seekers returned home as soon as they could afford to leave.

"The poor Indians have been treated with great cruelty, killed off without the slightest cause, and driven to starvation," related store owner Franklin A. Buck. Fortune hunters were reimbursed for their expenses by the California government when they raided unprotected Indian villages. Even the fish Indians used as food were driven from their streams as water was turned to mud by the miners.

But there were also some great success stories. Many gold finds were indeed spectacular, although a relatively tiny number of gold miners ended up with fabulous fortunes. The people who made out the best were usually merchants who "fleeced the Golden Fleecers" by selling necessities to miners at outrageous prices. One merchant is famous to this very day. Levi Strauss left a small, struggling business in New York and made millions when he stitched some sturdy pants for miners out of tenting material and began selling Levi jeans.

A German named Heinrich Schliemann traveled to California from Russia. He made a small fortune as a banker for customers he could address in eight languages, then returned to Europe and eventually became the archaeologist who discovered the ancient city of Troy. Leland Stanford, who later became a railroad magnate, a governor of California, a United States senator, and the founder of Stanford University, got his start with a share in a gold mine given to him instead of cash when he was a merchant in Sacramento. He later sold his interest for $400,000.

The California gold rush lasted barely a decade. When boom turned to bust after most of the easy-to-find gold was gone, big mining companies with money to spend on sophisticated equipment took over from the solitary prospector. Even though the rip-roaring days of adventure were over, many people decided not to leave for their former homes. Charmed by the beauty of the area and its offer of escape from the ordinary, they stayed in California, turned to farming or industry to make a living, and began to measure America's wealth by the bounty and vastness of its lands and not just the gold in its hills.

ASIA

PACIFIC OCEAN

Canton

Hawaiian Islands

AUSTRALIA

Sydney

NEW ZEALAND

ROUTES TO
California
BY LAND
& SEA

miles
0   1000   2000
0   1000   2000   3000
kilometers